Gallery Books
Editor Peter Fallon

HAWKS AND DOVES

Alan Gillis

HAWKS AND DOVES

Gallery Books

Hawks and Doves
is first published
simultaneously in paperback
and in a clothbound edition
on 17 May 2007.

The Gallery Press
Loughcrew
Oldcastle
County Meath
Ireland

www.gallerypress.com

ISBN 978 1 85235 417 6 *paperback*
        978 1 85235 418 3 *clothbound*

A CIP catalogue record for this book
is available from the British Library.

Contents

for Wendy

'Indoors the sound of the wind. Outdoors the wind.'
— Louis MacNeice, 'House on a Cliff'

The Mournes

Our heads plunged deep in BlackBerries,
TalkTalk, Anytime, Talk & Text and Flext
plans, it seems our senses are condemned
to a life sentence. And so, like Alice
through the mirror, Humpty-Dumpty men,
we try to piece ourselves back together again.

Under the steel sheet of a teal blue sky
we lose the city for the russet rills
and quiet of those heather-shagged mounds,
hunked and fallen crags that ruck and reel,
hollow and heave like the incredible body
of nobody living. Those hills do not peak

and poke the holed sky, but hold their bulk
defensively, ecstatically, or indifferently,
according to the weather. We burn in air-
conditioned cars through wafts of rosehip
and bone slurry, then park and walk
the dazzled razzle of Newcastle's strand,

where bare-bellied, wasp-buzzed children gorge
through comedy vampire teeth, George
and Tony masks, texting on clamshell phones,
tongues patrolling leaked honeycomb cones,
while gangs of girls sniggle and flirt
with a prism of Premiership football shirts.

We climb from the crush of bumper-
to-bumper cars into a cool-covered
river-hush of oaks and pines, then skift
the raised bogs of the lowlands

over the Brandy Pad to Hare's Gap
to gape at Bearnagh, Binnian, Lamagan,

Buzzard's Roost and Blue Lough Buttress.
We walk the wet heath and dry heath,
windlebrooke, darley dale, fiddler's gold
and blanket bogs of the uplands to where,
a cock-a-breeky with a catapult,
I'd tried to shoot down skylarks and linnets,

lapwings and tin cans, low helicopter
patrols and an endless stone wall.
Now nimble-hooved sheep ransack
the dwarf willow and starry saxifrage
on which we stop to slake our thirst,
take our bearings in the high bracing air.

We look over the Silent Valley, its gorges
and tors, the Slieves sloping, as ever before,
down to the wave-lipped and blue-burst
sea of trawlers, yachts, dinghies, and, too far
out for us to see, the milk-drops of dolphins,
cruisers, carriers, frigates gathering for war.

In her Room on a Light-kissed Afternoon

Not only the nip and tuck of her skin quilting
milk-bent bones; not only the somersaulting
head spin of her light skin spread atilt
the deep of her lemon-puffed pillow and quilt
lifting into the citron-charged air; but even the lilt
of strings from the speaker on her well-built
mockernut cabinet, the light from her half-
opened window and the high heckled laugh
of girls promenading past her bedroom,
scrickety-screeching over each other's lampoon
of a pizza-faced boy they tortured all afternoon;
even the snow-capped peaks of her importune
shoulder bones, the squidged soles of her feet,
the daylight's tufts in the meadowsweet
sky charged with godwits, lemon-puffed billows
and Boeings: all these things sink below
her ass-through-mouth fear of the aeroplane's *kaboom*,
its flaring nose dive-bombing her bedroom;
her fear of turning cloud, her skin become cotton,
a lemon-puffed pastry shred to pieces in the rotten
sky and wind blown, turned to tears
cut like arrowheads, salt-fired and clear,
pitter-patter-clattering her window
as I plunge her lip-stained pillow
and quilt, her light citrus skin
with hate mail, emissions, election results breaking in
as we lie there, beating, dead to our bones
in her lemon-puffed bower of words, and sticks, and stones.

You'll Never Walk Alone

She's dead set against the dead hand
of Belfast's walls guarding jinkered
cul-de-sacs, siderows, bottled sloganlands,
and the multinational malls' slicker
demarcations, their Xanadu of brands
entwining mind and income. Yet these replicas
atone for the brouhaha'd blare of the zones
she walks among, the bricked-in vigil of her home,

where they axed and hacked bark-stripped trees
and razed grass clearings, piled varnish-caked
crates and oil-slick tyres to a fire and stoned
dark-skinned refugees, broke Bacardi-Breezer
empties off kerbstones, paint-bombed windows,
raised their spray cans to new tenements,
built-up cans and butts like battlements
outside her door, and dreamed of burning green,
white and orange to ribbons that would rave
and rip through the dawn's zit of orange.

She walks by Little Britain merchandise,
made in China, and waits like a leper
in the darkened corridor of a debt advice
counsel room, listening to gangsta rappers
rapping that days slip by like grains of rice,
so she should shake her booty; that she is tapered
by time; that she should shed another skin;
that some days trampoline, flipping you outside-in.

'Such was the day' — I later heard her say,
soused in gin or doused with fontal waters
fallen from the apple-sliced, orange-peeling sky,
her shadow flaked as she wrangled for just

words — 'such was the day, not when guerrillas
ate the protestors' livers before a village
crowd for opposing oil drills on TV;
nor when the bright lights flared over Baghdad's
orange, rose and *Tomb Raider* blue targets
trained by oil wells firing a welcome, or adieu;

nor when the dawn green ocean's heart attack
churned coastlines into troughs of corpse-stew;
when the earthquake turned tenements to smokestacks;
but the day I broke down and bawled myself blue
by my front door's graffiti, falling on the cracked,
coloured kerb with every bill overdue,
wishing the ground would gobble me whole, and
a neighbour asked if I needed a hand.'

For What We Are About To Receive

Five million to one are the odds
against pulling fish for five thousand
from these two loins I bought from the reduced to clear
stall at the snubbed end of the pine-
fresh mall, so I'd have money left over
for five Belfast baps and twelve green

bottles of beer, although the green
splotch of the loins might stack the odds
against wanting such wonders to be worked over
their flesh in any case, even if it were to feed five thousand
gathered under alder and pine
to hear the Word spelled out loud and clear,

just as you laid down the law that night I bought clear
spring water and readymade greens
that I sprinkled with toasted pine
nuts as you spelled out loud and clear that the odds
against us keeping faith were five thousand
to one, and that I needed to get over

the fact that we were over.
And just as when the Word was spelled out loud and clear
and the herded five thousand
set their teeth into twelve green
creels full of fragments and fish and ends and odds
left from the dais under alder and pine,

now I chew over my five Belfast baps and pine
for your loins forevermore, picking over
fragments, ends and odds
and leftovers I'll never clear

away as I splutter on my twelfth green
bottle amid breadcrumbs in their thousands

watching fifty, one hundred, two hundred thousand
loincloths on my pine-
framed TV, coming over pukey-green
as I work the figures over and over
until it's spelled out loud and clear
that five million to one are the odds

against anyone feeding those five hundred thousand spread
    like odds
and ends who pine for bread and clear
spring water, their skin gangrened, the broadcast over.

Saturday Morning

The fart and snigger of sausages and free
range eggs, the beans of a coffee grinder
and light house music on a Fujifilm CD
blank out of mind the mortuary white-
yellow shake of your hands, the humming
tube of your kitchen's fluorescent light.

Hitachi diggers stack roots, earth and scree
into mountains, then abandon them
to slouch indifferently over traffic heard
charging from the city like buffalo
stampeding towards Burger Kings in the country,
family estrangements, malls of born-again logos.

Foamy-chopped dogs frisk the pavements
for barf-free kebab or hot dropped fry,
mobiles trilling de-daw-de-dee theme tunes,
their birdsong jukeboxing the cigarette air
as rain falls from a plum sky on taxis
hunting for knickered, knackered, come-down fares.

You sing a little, the music and pork fingers
oozing through you until backwashed in blue
half-slips, red halternecks and voluptuary
ankle braids, the armpits of the night
criss-crossed in car parks and harbours,
your thub-a-dub-dub turned ting-a-ling-ding.

You slab on the sofa's shucking leather:
advice on contemporary interiors
hmms from a tube-lit screen as you raft
into waterdark, your parts equidistant,

tacked with Pritt Stick or with UHU glue —
the you who is there, and the you who isn't.

You are happy when the room disappears,
when the dull glass drizzles into static,
then flicks to the colours of Columbo
or The World and you ogle live stars,
interact with talent or violent nature
shows, teenage models launching their memoirs.

In open fields unleashed men belt
leather balls with bootlaces, foaming,
dribbling and colliding under a throne
of purple fire, riotous in jockstraps
below on-gushing winds. By covered rivers
they are casting flies, watching the ripple-laps.

In pools they dunk into public water
kowtowing to children hung off their necks
while you ooze through your own dibble-dapple
letting thought-bubbles lather your head,
lolling into whirlpools and suds
to sink and skim your lichened riverbed.

Where a grey wave hammer-walled
through the costal village an orange
Clio is perched on a green wych elm.
Click. On arctic chops a black and mammoth
keel welts into a beluga, its blood
staining the floes like sweet vermouth.

Click. A celebrity chef provides fresh ideas
for sausages. Click. The merlin falls like a brick

on a bank vole's head. Click. The President.
Click. The pop star peels down to his gonads.
Click. 'Oh my God, look at her kitchen!' Click.
Janjaweed teenagers patrol the road to Chad.

Outside the wind shushes shivering trees
rising with the whine of a worried hairdryer
into the bow-wow whooshing of a sonic jet-stream
overhead as a plane flickers on the canvas
of overwhelming blue, stringing its vapour trails
to Ho Chi Minh City or the green plains of Kansas.

If you lie there long enough you'll grow roots
deep in the sofa's core, your face swarming
into pixels, a hodgepodge of static
sucked into thin air or gobbled by worms
of underground cable to be spewed out
on a screen in the office of an advertising firm.

Lie there long enough and you will drown
in the glut-stream of yourself, or nothing,
as you dissolve into the screen, its thin lips
gaping into such a maw you cannot undo
its babbling hoodoo. Lie back long enough
in your caramel dream and the sky will spew

down leatherwood trees and livestock,
scudding waves rising, the gobbledegook
wind no longer passing, plates colliding,
green plains flooded as children in nylon
splish-splash and wade through a dreamtime
torrent of branches, bikes, pillows, pylons

flowing down the submerged terraced street
until hauled by their parents onto rooftops
to feed the ducks by chimney pots.
'Brush both sides so it doesn't stick.'
Click. The President. Click. 'And the lucky
winner is.' Click. 'I've always loved you.' Click.

'The future is Orange.' The gas fire of the sun
will raze the savannahs that remain,
their open fields a torture victim's tongue
pulled out and fag-burnt and blistered to bubble-
wrap with ants writhing over skeletons sprawled
as if they'd been making love, or playing Twister.

Outside pensioners slouch towards hospital
wards and their partners, or blank rooms without
partners as the men return refreshed from
their combat. And with a custard finger
you flick on *Deep Rider* in which the hero, Randy,
hump-humps his American humdinger

in blue car parks and harbours, his pallid
cheeks lit by water-light. Blank out of mind
the hum rising up behind the flickering glass,
hissing and sniggering through the crevasse
of your smug and peeling sofa's leather.
A new show's beginning. Pull yourself together.

Sunday Lunch

He's in the Congo, the Sahara, crossing the wild
Texan plains as he buffets in his chair,
Skip the kangaroo springing in his eye,
his hair sprung like a radio tower
transmitting coded messages from Mars.
He gawks and gawps at the torture of turnips
and will never sit at peace, his pockets packed
with spiders, Spitfires, galleons, red-hot cars.

She sighs as he clums her side again,
always back-snashed, tending to
the nut-brown and cherry bobble of her hair.
A spick and span kitchen of her own gleams
in her eye. She's tottering at a high gate,
both pushed towards the chameleon
city's skylights and pulled back into the valley,
the family's arms. She is three weeks late.

Her mum straightens the salt cellar with her
bi-weekly cut and blow-dried autumn red bomb-
scare hair, the jabble and jibble of the kitchen
glinting through the jade of her eye.
She's zonked, and hears the cold pull of waters
flowing beyond the valley, hills, the horizon,
wondering what her husband might do
and who to shelter if their daughter drops the bomb.

He sits there, flare-nosed, cragged-eared,
mealy-mouthed, breadwinning for the table,
stale fire and flint-blue justice in his eye,
guerrilla hair defeating oil and comb.
He stares at the table or lifts his hand
to bark about who in the town is broke

and who is dead. The rest of the table plead
for the Grace of God. He brows his head.

Then two more face each other unnoticed.
Who knows what horrid image has unfixed
his hair, while hers is a hand-sculpted bath
for birds. If addressed, they speak of gardens
or fish, whatever the question is. She shakes
in her scarf, he quakes in his tie. They eat
like birds while the river runs beyond the valley,
hills, horizon, the bale harvest of their eyes.

To What I Did Thou Show'dst Me First The Way

1

Not so much born as given forth
by an angel, who disappeared
up a burnt offering, he was raised in a land
that lay under the hand of Philistines for forty years.

2

He walked up to his mummy and daddy
with a twelve-inch Bowie knife:
'I saw a Philistine woman at Timnah,
now get her for me as my wife.'

3

After tearing the lion, as the lion
tears the kid, after bees honeycombed
the belly of that corpse, he gobbled a scoop,
funny-honey-slobbering fingers and chin.

4

When the people saw him they brought
thirty companions to be with him.
For their thirty festal garments thirty
men would be torn limb from limb.

5

Zigzagged lightning, or birds of fire?
What's that skreighing in the night and razing

our homes? Three hundred crazed foxes he's set
on farm and field, their bushy tails blazing.

6

Then the spirit of the Lord rushed on him,
something dropped from eyes long blind,
and he boned a thousand foreskins to death
as he completed his partial mind.

7

In her dark and gold tent she goes down
with forked tongue. He smiles. Ah!
The hookah, the rings and bells,
the henna-limned thighs of Delilah!

8

With painted eyes and that troubling tongue
she nagged and moaned and pleaded and read
the riot act until he wished he was dead.
Then she cropped the fatal harvest of his head.

9

Eyeless in Gaza, he suffered
dysentery in chains, and heard rats
writhe in darkness, the Philistine cries:
'Simmer down, big man. Dry yer eyes!'

10

What happened next, you know:
As with the force of winds and waters pent,
When mountains tremble, those two massy pillars
With horrible convulsion to and fro

11

He tugged, he shook, till down they came and drew
The whole roof after them, with burst of thunder
Upon the heads of all who sat beneath,
Lords, ladies, captains, counsellors, or priests.

12

His father built a monument in the shade
of laurel to praise his enemies' mourning.
Across the land, the fruits of his sacrifice rise
in burnt offerings every morning.

There

Scooshing by barrels in brewers' yards,
by the Enterprise ratcheting southward;
spanging over downs of such avocado green
you check yourself, and through elmwood demesnes
that canopy civil servants in the twilight;
scudding the dark between bulbs of light
pollution, past lynchets, bales and unstill horses,
the rain-soaked lough, the detachment of houses;

slacken at the clutter of an outspilling town:
there flues and scaffolding, run-down
chemists and redevelopment clearance sites,
car parks and faded posters of kick-boxing fights
occupy hooded teens, the question marks
of their clusters, their murmur more dark
than passers-by can account for, on their way to
late night malls, the news, convenience drive-throughs —

the till ka-chinging demographic, who'd like to cycle
more in the future, who drive miles to recycle
and buy organic, passing value-pack fish fingers
purchased for scuzzed children, whose eyes linger
on the shelf-bright colours, leaving by flexi-bus
for estates on the outskirts, complexes of window dust
beyond the CCTV zones, where high-walled shadows
veil adjoining green fields, their symmetrical hedgerows

revealing the depth of order. There WAY OUT signs
rust quietly. There dead leaves bare the trees' design,
thorn bushes sharpen, militant jackdaws shiver
on thin wires, policing the lash-cackled river;
and past a station post, its generator's hum,

the lough sluiced pebbles, an ulcered tongue
slivered over loose teeth. There you must earn your living:
locked in food chains, frigid skylines unforgiving.

Wasps

I took a ferry to Belfast and ducked
and lipped the saltwater grains
whipped up in its wake to ogle
as machines and fields grew bigger
where the wet newspaper print of Belfast
swarmed into focus like porridge
and strawberries bowled by the green
rocked rump and hump of hills.

I saw the jungle or gymnasium
of cranes, slips and pulleys, the mangle
of rusted hulks, iron mammoths
still prowling with wan malice
over the dockyard's dun immensity
as the water treacled and brined
around the fudged ferry chugging
carbon flukes to berth in the slime.

I took my blue Picasso or Civic east
bypassing the Odyssey, Oval
and Tesco-Sainsbury stand-off
under landing planes and take-offs
chugging up a clogged artery
over green-rocked lump-and-frumped hills
where clouds dolloped another town's
bowl of porridge and strawberry.

I called again for you but you were back
at the docks on a weekend shift
so I stalked the old hunting grounds,
bluebell-blared slopes hid by tall
nettles and fern where an amber-fizzed bee
helicoptered her lilac elastic

waistband holding everything up —
when a bee monsoon helled over us.

I ran with her through tall nettles
and ferns away from bees or wasps
catherine-wheeling after the red
lemonade bottle I missiled direct-
hit their honeycomb of terror,
thorns barbed-wiring our snow-haired shins
tripped by low stalks to stumble down
green-rocked hills tripping ankle over chin.

You were on the east rim of the city's
hardly-manned docks or dungeons
working the oil storage facility
harbour for rust-hulled boats
funnelling the black dragon trapped
coiled in low tankers, seething
to be fire-engine electrical light
to ignite the hooked buildings of Belfast.

I clambered down the hill to the estate
where she said she wouldn't be coming out
again for the foreseeable future —
where a hive of us played Twister
on NO BALL GAMES greens that were brown —
and saw mince fried fingers and petunias
bunched in a burned-out wheelie-bin's
industrial piss-stench of bluebottle din.

You were keeper of the flame and dealer,
dragon-tamer, quiet watcher of lough
water and weather waiting to offload

dark money-juice to mainliners
dragon-chasing through the country's
civic industrial and military veins
to turn them on and keep turning over
until a dragon boat came dockward again.

I almost chucked and lost myself
a little to pissing in public
phone boxes, raw egg and potatoes,
Razzles in ruins doused with paraffin,
Telegraphs, Wyatt and Woolf, sinister
checkpoint peelers with cauliflower
ears, crocus noses and a falling
hibiscus soothing Dicky's dick twisters.

You docked them in and clocked them out,
catastrophic steel keels belching
venom in tide-locked tar-water
in every weather dwarfing your yellow-
coated black-smudged persistence with pipes
and pressure levels making extreme
mood swings of wind, wave and tonnage
tick over — a souped-up machine.

I almost found myself in an Escort
with boom-boom speakers and Johnny
Darkness, nutted nose and temple thuds,
speeding window views in a stew;
with orange haddock and white sauce,
ginger fingers, Berkeleys and Bensons
as I pandered to her rustle and lime-
stretched blouse under shaken oleander.

You slumped back in the boxed office,
all in your care well looked after
but needling — mouths never filled —
and dreamed your way back on low boats,
salt winds and fumes in your throat
under a swarming black yellow-starred sky
on coral seas or the ever unfolding
Pacific's killer whale-stitched cloak.

I had left that town of darkness
full of a darkness of my own
so many times this time I took
forever going over the green-rocked
hills' drop and climb with my Civic's
windows open, chasing the valley fall's
blue slopes and fern banks, gilt and diesel
clouds towards Belfast's open terminals.

You packed up after all this time
and left behind the harbour forever
where it's likely we passed on the water-
edged carriageway under herring-gull cries
watching catamarans and long
low tankers float into figments of
strawberry drops and ink blots
on the lough-water's incredible sky.

Bob the Builder is a Dickhead

Some night when you're lost in a nest of narrow lanes
and you've forgotten where you're from, where you're going,
 again,

you'll think back and thank me for when you were three
and I threw out all of your Bob the Builder DVDs.

I'm telling you now — Scoop, Dizzy, Lofty,
Muck and Rolly will make you soft and we

can't have you thinking you can fix it
every time the fan is hit with flying horseshit.

They want you to believe you should work for the team,
sacrifice yourself to a starched-collar dream,

but here's your choice: be shat upon or look out for No. 1;
either kick against the pricks, or else become one.

Balamory's full of Torys! Silence the Fat Controller
imposing his order on the island of Sodor!

But don't go bawling, this isn't Doomsday,
it's simply better things are spelled out this way.

For example, sex.
Pick up what you can at the local multiplex,

for soon your sanity will rely on
how well you placate your wee pyjama python.

Soon you'll do anything for your love's furry mouse,
so take her to Paris, or your favourite curry house

and buy her a lamb balti with a Cobra or Tiger,
rub her happy thigh as you sit down beside her,

but fastforward the scene by a couple of years
and you'll have nothing but Yesterday between your ears.

She'll have left you hopped-up, gormless, parched,
just one more wrinkle on the arse.

You'll want to whisk back on a magical broom
to that mystic split-second of your fusion in the womb:

to fly through celestial chaos, that cosmic hootenanny,
and find the divine factory where they sort out pricks from
    fannies.

There, you'll seek the management office in order to destroy
the Goddess of Creation — who'll be announcing over the
    tannoy

with flat-packed officiousness:
'Welcome, customers! On entering consciousness,

please proceed directly to an impasse and fill
out a complaint form.' For this is Mission Impossible:

think positive, think negative — whatever you reckon,
your thoughts will self-destruct in fifteen seconds.

You'll end up on your knees seeking Holy Communion,
a taxpaying citizen of a multinational union.

Your American landlord will swing by in his Lexus,
take all your money, then fuck off back to Texas.

You might move from place to place, a mind-boggled rover,
or stay in Belfast where, although the war is over,

the Party of Bollocks and the Party of Balls
are locked in battle for the City Hall.

Even if you roam, you'll find it difficult
to avoid starvation and its twin, the cult

of profit backed by death planes firing vanity,
variable rates, trigger-fingered inanity.

But, of course, I might be wrong. Perhaps a constant
path exists for the fearless itinerant

to tread where, on the threshold of heaven,
the figures on the street become the figures of heaven

and our ears will alloy the preposterous babble.
One thing's for sure, every step will be a gamble.

Will it be paper, scissors, or stone?
Take another throw, son, of the devil's bones.

These Things That Are Given

But once did she say your mother
rules your roost and you must leave her,
or live forever in the nightmare
of your making. But once I left her.
Sphagnum moss feazed the air.
I walked until enormous and dead
humps poked from their underwear
of hazel and vetch, the sky bled,
a frampling tongue of fog slurred
over pine and sycamore heads.
And I was that mist clung to the burl
of myself, shrouding the forge
in the sky, where I slowly unfurled,
an egg wrapped in gilt and orange.

The Lights

Green is for go and red for going no-
where as my brother drums his fingers in
a rhythm on my head. Sister says
the lights and he takes up the wheel,
turning left and driving through a rainbow
coalition of well-heeled mannequins
in hyper-lit titillated go-go displays,
burnt homes under boarding and real
deal posters frayed upon bookies and bars
in which I'd embark upon a fifteen-year binge
to block out this advice in the car
filled with sun, a honey-centred lozenge:
buck yourself up, don't you know you are . . .
He breaks off. The lights are orange.

Carnival

Black buffed leather-tongued brogues with oat-
meal socks and khaki Y-fronts, pleated slacks,
pert navy and gold striped double-windsored tie
on a twill non-iron white hassle-free shirt,
stiff blazer, wool felt bowler, dead white
gloves and orange sash with silver tassels,
marching onward, left, right, elbows tight
to Lambegs, banners, fifes, rows of waving
wives, marching onward, in formation, marching
on a Judas nation by the Queen's highway,
the town's High Street, roundabouts where forked
roads meet and never yield, marching to the field
of battle, field of peace, field patrolled by plain-
clothed police; field of Jesus, field of hope, field
of Bush and Fuck the Pope; marching onward into
heaven to scourge its halls of unwashed brethren;
then a blue bus home, content with your labours,
to watch *Countdown* and your favourite, *Neighbours*.

Neighbours

The day fills with day-care centres.
Men bet in wards and download
scenes of Jordan. A big dealer
chews the face off a schoolgirl.

My neighbour clanks off
for a dark rum snifter and can
of sardines as the woman down
the street walks her daughter
to the bus, Berkeley streaming,
wishing she could work,
wishing she could be her daughter
when her hairdryer becomes
a microphone and her bed
of dolls turns to the Odyssey.

My neighbour sloothers back,
front door left ajar, as if waiting
for a visit, slicing cheddar
by streaming coupons with
a key-ring knife, talking
to a photograph of his wife.

Home and Away

Fuckin Billy came home the night before for all
the fuckin world as if he'd been to Magaluf,
yawping and bullocking through the front fuckin hall
as we were taking the fuckin table from the roof-
space with the wobbly fuckin leg I was to see to.
He dropped his fuckin bags, showed off his new tattoos,
gave Pat a big fuckin schmoocher, and with that scabby
fuckin grin bulldozed up the stairs with Debbie.
Next day Tony was wrapped up in a fuckin new
Union Jack with wee Markie decked out in a fuckin blue
blazer and me in my black fuckin pin-striped suit
while Pat was a picture having dyed her fuckin roots
back to the colour she fuckin had before William died
(after that she hadn't worked, her house fuckin ashtrayed
and she was taken to a fuckin home for the head-fried
for a year — now, no one fuckin mentions it). Anyway,
Billy and Debbie looked like fuckin Burton and Taylor,
Sonny and fuckin Cher, though it was clear as day
he'd beat thirty fuckin shades of blue shite out of her
if he fuckin knew she'd been playing away
from home when he was fuckin bolted up inside.
Lined up by the fuckin sandwiches, we embraced
women from up and down the fuckin street who packed
the room in tight fuckin clothes, and all was braced
for a jar-full, some song, a fuckin belly-full of crack
and, you never know, the chance of a fuckin ride —
but wee fuckin Markie was all over the place
and our Billy had to take him to one fuckin side
to explain the way things work. Fucker even tried
to claim he'd be fuckin proud if *his* Da had died.

The Lad

I spend my days drinking beneath
the bar's plasma screen, checking out
the Czech waitress, all tits and teeth.
And when I hear someone splitting hairs,
antsy with a world of cares about the rights
and wrongs of the war, or whether
the fulltime score fairly reflected the game,
I wade in and tell them 'pity the man
unsure of his name', then leave them
to brood, secure in my manhood.

I pay my way, walk out to the car park,
and with my right hand I grip my Adam's whip,
my hazel wand, my straw-haired vagabond,
my Pirate of Penzance, my lilac love lance,
my ramrod, my wad, my schlong, my tube, my tonk,
my Jimmy, my Johnny, my tarse, my verge, my honk,
my bishop, my pawn, my rook, my king, my knight,
my Gonzo, my Kermie, my Bert, my Ernie,
my chairman of the board, my stranger in the night,
my weenie, my weener, my Mr Misdemeanour,

my chopper, my boffer, my chantilly lace-loving big bopper,
my porridge pipe, my yellow and ripe
banana, my iguana, my nerve-ends of Nirvana,
my snuffer, my chuffer, my duffer, my stuffer,
my Black and Decker, my donut inspector,
my dickery-dock, my Geronimo's tomahawk,
my tinkle, my sprinkle, my Rip Van Winkle,
my Mad Max, my Crazy Mick, my dip-, my wiggle-, my
    pogo-stick,
my hawk, my dove, my love-
bomb bazooka, my squinty-eyed scheming pooka,

my Chief Whip, my guv, my middle man in the transactions
   of love,
my hootchie-cootchie tickler, my sporty little ripper,
my virginia creeper, my heat seeker,
my Best, my Law, my Charlton, my Stiles,
my volatile erstwhile fertile mobile projectile,
my d'Artagnan, my explorer of the canyon,
my saxophone, my knick-knack-paddy-whack, my dog and
   my bone,
my saucisson, my saveloy, my knackwurst, my donger,
my Pinocchio's nose growing longer, and longer,
my high and flighty piccolo, my 'just popped out to say hello',

my Hans Solo, my Marco Polo, is this the way to Amarillo?,
my zoot-suited rooter, my hooter, my trusty pee-shooter,
my custard marrow, my Zeno's arrow, my submarine
   descending the abyssal plain's narrows,
my Emperor Ming, my Lord of the Rings,
my pintle, my pizzle, my bringer of the drizzle,
my Spade, my Holmes, my Marlowe, my Wimsey,
my dawn-raid, my dome, my sparrow, my flip-flop-flimsy,
my sweet disorder in the dress, my six million dollar man
   (more or less),
my Viceroy, my land ahoy, my wild colonial boy,
my noble Lord issuing like Radiant *Hesper* when his golden
   hayre in th'*Ocean* billowes he hath Bathed fayre,

my busker in the subway, my folk singer, my ring-a-ling-a-
   ding-dong-dinger,
my tomatoes and cucumber, my lucky bingo number,
my blubber, my flubber, my slippy-dippy rubberdubber,
my pepperoni rollarama, my wildebeest grazing on the
   plains of the savannah,

my great rooted blossomer, my limp father of thousands,
my bearded iris that brought forth buds, and bloomed blossoms,
   and yielded almonds,
my curious Hobbit, my John Wayne Bobbit;
and with my goose-pimpled bum against my Nissan's bonnet,
my one-eyed zipper fish blows an angel's kiss
as I hit-and-miss into the tax disc of the sun.

Strangers

I bought my house off Bill,
his hair all Brylcreem slicks,
who had moved there when
he was seventeen with six

brothers and sisters, his folks
at each other's throats, and he told me
they were in care homes now
and kept mistaking him for Harry,

the eldest, who left for Perth
and nobody knows from Adam,
and he carped on forever, then said
he'd picked a new house at random

because he couldn't wait to be shot
of this place, its long rope of ghosts.
So I tried to strip the walls but there
were too many layers, each a milepost

into muzzed sub-histories, and I ended
up brushing over the botched
job with a bone-white budget
gloss leaving a semolina of splotch

and divot on the walls. Then I
bought my bed and began to sleep
on the sofa, where I feel
less coffined as cheap

paint peels off mashed potato
walls and daddy-long-legs trawl

pocked linoleum, skirting boards,
scudded rooms welled with the vitriol

of past lives spent riding out
what rhythm could be found within
these walls. I lie back to study
the lunar tarpaulin

of the ceiling, its curds and whey,
its flirtation with collapse,
when runty whiffs ladle from no-
where to perch in the apse

of my nose and a burnt hum
of toast and swamp of grey eggs
insults the room. Then I hear
a piston of nettle-stung legs

and verruca'd feet splash in
the slanging of a shared Sunday
bath, skin sloshed under sheets
of thwacked laundry.

I nuzzle my head deeper
in my splay of fuzzed
cushions, sailing further
into the scuffed room's buzzed

undersound of snorting pipes,
drafts, street-yammers
blending with the cistern's
skin-crawling grammar

that tunes into voices taunting
with things said or done
or not said, undone; injuries
that cannot be healed or unspun

back upon the jenny of my tongue
with the clangers, whoppers,
porky pies seasoned with spite
that now come a cropper,

every night in this bone-
white room. And I chew
over getting in touch as distant
telephones to-whit, to-whoo,

to suggest we sit together
for a peace pipe and powwow.
But I need to get on with things,
and we are different people now.

Morning Emerges out of Music

We dip, drop and dovetail in a cabaret
with crushed daiquiris and spellbound
maracas clippety-clapping the way
words click together and channel their sound
to a gorge-drop, a doorway, the sky-top's
blue veil. But then alarm bells ring, the music stops,
and I wake to a fade-out, an aftersound
of bebblers behind a curtain of air
that I chase through, my head dancing around
after rhythms without meaning, without care.

Chalk and Cheese

She says: 'If I'm the barley, you're the hoe.'
Ho-ho. But no, between us, I often wonder,
who's the spellbound nation, who's the Führer.
She says: 'If I'm the fresh lime in the punch-bowl
of our love, you're the bitter tang of angostura.'
And when I was dragged to a darkened corridor
and found myself turning into, to my horror,
a gingered pulp of tallow and skin-rot
with bone-splintered, vein-burst, after-death eyes
she said: 'Love, come away from the mirror.'

Among the Barley

1

We met at the tail of a check-out queue
and when she turned her head she spread
like blood through snowflakes, all melt and fire,
as my ripe tomatoes tumbled to the floor.
And when she bared her chamomile thighs,
her red-toed sunblaze, my body became
barley fields on fire. My frazzled ears roared.
My old house flared to fizz-burned bananas,
red meat frizzle-zings, the attic razed to hell,
and I knelt at the doorway singing High Hosannas.

2

After she'd cut her door key and laid out
blueprints of her kitchen cupboards' insides
I felt deep-bosomed, big-bellied and wide
as a turnip field, days before harvest.
I bought walking boots and walked through river-
wound groves. I bought allegories of birth
and death, framed them, and drilled them to
her wall. And how they fell. When she entered
a room eyes swivelled and bulged for her,
red crab-apples craving for the earth.

3

For you I wanted to leaf and take root.
So I stood firm and pulled my lips full gape,
wanting to mouth apples. *Uaugghh.* I *uaugghh*ed
nothing until it hurt. And then I surrendered.
Orchards of apples began to appear —

pear-shaped, plum-coloured, pineapple-dappled.
My eyes turned seed, my veins fructosed,
and my mouth bloomed stem-twigs for sound
and wounded fruit for sense, gulping forth
a juiced-up speech, or merely talking apples.

4

I slap a second lick of banana dream gloss
on the back room's walls while you measure
the cove for hanging your unframed mirror.
Soon we'll discuss diaries, looking for
windows when we can next DIY together.
The forecast is for spells of lower pressure.
I finger-slick sweat from your pent shoulders
as the sun leaks onto the living-room floor
to trickle down thighs and thrawn limbs —
barley sheaves waiting for the thresher.

5

We walk a line that curves from day
to day, often squiggly, higgledy-piggledy,
as if etch-a-sketched by a sugar-rushed
two-year-old, so that I find myself
rushing through a maze of malls, esplanades,
restaurants, barley fields, beds, lakeside
paths and patios with legendary sundials —
meeting points that blend and deepen
and brighten and bloom the way a room
looks bigger when you've been in it for a while.

6

We meant to make love on the stairs,
the desk chair, the windowsill, the throw
your sister brought back from Brazil.
Now we zigzag and busy-buzz by
one another like honeybees snuffing
pollen in the autumnal red and gold glare.
So let our love be watertight and let
the breeze blow through it. Let us be solid
oak and fluid. Let us be truth, let us be dare,
the swallow's dive sculpted into rock, and air.

Driving Home

I saw it coming, as I zipped and vroomed
headward from Coleraine to Belfast
under phone masts and sycamores
arching the flat road's tunnel through
hayfields, sun-gilt and harvests, my red
car careening in a fifth gear of freedom
past other cars' carbon fart trails,
cloudsmoked brushstrokes over scumbled
green horizons, every driver shooting
the bluetooth breeze with front windows
rolled to share their iPods' perfect playlists.

I saw it coming, as I left behind
the office and to-do lists; my boss, my other
boss, the other one again; that one's manager;
high priority email and enlarge your man-
hood spam; battery chicken, leathered ham pie;
visions of efficiency and a potted peace
lily that I'll have to water next time;
workmates eroticizing over calling it quits;
workmates swearing their colleagues are drooped shits;
squirly-whirlies on paper; the toilet floor *Star*;
a prissy car-park barrier blocking the car.

I saw it coming, loopy-go-lucky
muff-eared tongue-wagging happy-
as-sunlight mutt with scutched fawn coat:
a hop-skip-tittuping half-labrador
in a swagger chasing its own moist snout
filled with wonder, careening from sidepath
to roadway in a slavered rabbit dream,
leaving me two seconds to size up
I couldn't brake because the pimped-up

Micra up my ass was too near, too fast —
Dumph! It tail-chased death throes in the wing-
mirror spinning mad and bad-moon howling

out of sight. I'd no end of time to stop
but never did as the Micra overtook me,
for I might have had to carry that hyper-
ventilating half-corpse or matted carcass
with fleas and nothing in its eyes
up some farmyard lane to a child or sour
culchie into *Deliverance* and, anyway,
I wanted to get home to eat and channel-
surf for something decent or close my eyes
and drown in my sofa, so I hammered
headward down that road of sun and hay.

I va-va-voomed but the dog kept spinning
although left long behind, whirligigging
in a rear view of my mind so I couldn't
avert my eyes from that spinning jenny
death-dervish below the sky churning
buttermilk, lobster, apricot and kale.
The flat road lined with moonwort demanded
I turn back — but then I'd have to confess
I'd gone on for thirteen miles under pricked pines
hounding me, making me want to shunt
up to race-speed and take-off past the police
lurched with speed guns behind the '30' sign.

I might have pulled over and left
my car's front doors flung openwide —
a rickety carrier abandoned by picnic
tables in a litterblown parking bay

awaiting its lost passengers' return —
and hurled myself over the hedge to roam
google-eyed through deergrass and junipers
under a vanilla-rippled sky of crab shell,
tarragon and kelp to find a runnel
fleeced with bittercress and agrimony
where I'd lie and let the water-pepper
or salt-grass finger through me.

As I lay by the leak and lint of that runnel,
blaeberries and zigzag clover riddling
through me under puma-skinned skies,
I might have looked over the mantilla
of sheaves, stooks and stubble strewn across
that landscape of labrador downs,
or rolled beneath a yew to catch its leaves
contrailed by cream-slathered clouds
over the earth turning slowly around;
I might have lain and let flitter-fluttered birds
build their hay-nests in my eye-bowls
by the gash of that distant carriageway.

I might have drifted off, crossed over lanes
to collide in a slipstream of coming
and going, never here nor there but up
in the air, chasing homeward where to-do
lists are lurking, waiting for night to flip
my fried mind over until morning's
automatic return to the car and journey
back to that withered fantail of online
satellite navigation and in-car 3D
lapdance simulation, along those pointillist

phone masts and sycamores still arching
the road's bore through sun-gilt and harvest.

When I finally steered and veered the bend
into Belfast and turned into my street
I could have killed for a takeaway
but it was my turn to take the boy's
fire engine, fluffy dog and laser gun
to bed where we lay below his globed atlas lamp,
self-timed to fade, rotating projected
continents on the borderlined walls'
night-blue planetarium, where we read
until drift-off into nothing, unmoored
from the axled turn and low-watt embers
of the earth's spinning top left long behind.

After Arcadia

Nature lovers freed on heathered mountains . . .
Weekenders on a spin through clovered valleys . . .
Arm-linked lovers disappearing into forests . . .
Give your ears to this gabble-clinkered music
that chitters my wits all through the claggy morning
and skitters my senses until whiskey snigs the night.

You in the airplane, candescent through the night
over high-rises, pylons, beacon towers, mountains . . .
You in the ferry come to harbour in the morning . . .
You in the train scuttling through linden valleys . . .
Give your ears to this gabble-clinkered music
that's made of my mind a fungus-festered forest.

I used to potter and pootle, fribble through the forest
free from fear of the heat of the sun. Through the night
with friends I played doo-wop or boogie-woogie music
but now the days are lined up like streeled mountains
of shit, the nights are thunder-blanched valleys,
and my mind's a smashed window in the morning.

I used to be a rat up a rhododendron in the morning
having dreamed myself post-coital in a forest
or viburnum- and broom-blazed valley
with Emmanuelle Béart. Now after grogged nights
climbing out of bed is like climbing a mountain
as the radio squawks cockatoo-cawed, cock-a-doodle music.

Long since this jerk-jarred, clinkered, cockalorum music
has screeched like a cat clamped by a pit-bull in the morning
as though its dentist's drill and frogged bass could level
    mountains.
Long since my mind's been tree-stumped, a cleared forest.

Long since the cuckoo and curlew, nightingale and night-
jar have been silenced; the suburbs have long seized every valley.

Long since the burger-eating burghers of bright suburban
    valleys
ordered me to lay off this cockamamie-chorded music
because it disrupted their day's work and upset their night.
Long since I hate the night, the day, the morning.
Long since feral panthers hunt me through the forest
of my mind until I wish I lay under heathered mountains.

It seems to me I've seen thunder-rocked mountains
turn to burdocked, blasted, gridironed, gridlocked valleys.
It seems to me all I hear in the fubbed and fashed forest
of my mind is hippo-squealing, monkey-cackled music.
It seems to me every coffee bean and raspberry morning
hemlocks into narked, nixed, nulled and naggled night.

It seems to me I see a coal-choked and coughing night
as soon as the morning sun yokes over gorse-buttered
    mountains.
It seems to me I smell draggled offal-dregs in the morning
when I whiff the well-kempt gardens of the valley.
It seems to me I hear, when I seek river music,
the skreak of troops torture-training in the forest.

Every laurel, larch, birch, pine, poplar in the forest;
all lovers, single-drinkers, kerb-crawlers in the night;
each horn-blowing, finger-plucking finder-out of music;
all nature lovers, river-gargles, kestrels in the mountain;
each bungalow, weeping-willow, ivy-walled garden in the valley;
every cock-crow, kettle-call, car ignition in the morning

turns me scutched and scatty, buckety-bananas in the
    morning,
bidding me strike a match and blow, fireball the forest
of my mind more low-down than the lowest, meanest valley.
Every night I hope to see, no more, the star-scrappled night.
I'm midge-bitten, car-crashed with shame in sight of
    mountains,
buckarooed and buckled by that gobble-gabbled music.

For you've been taken, and the staff and bars of music,
all scale and concord, taken with you. The morning
sun in keeping time mocks mountains
and makes fair game of pines, these pricks, this forest.
Even the night's a cover version of a more primal, final night,
as security lights switch off-and-on in the clustered valley.

You would say that we are lights dimming in the valley;
that we're bound for harvest, a diminuendo in the music
of ourselves. No need for gnashed teeth in the night.
See the ferry come to harbour in the morning . . .
See arm-linked lovers return from quiet forests . . .
It's as if one might yet hold forth with valleys, music,
    mountains.

But you are under heathered mountains, and the clovered
    valleys
and covered forests are kirved by that gabble-gobbled music
that chitters the morning and skitters my sore-stung night.

A Blueprint for Survival

I don't know you, you don't know me,
but if we want to carry on we need
to make like mountaineers who tie themselves
together to survive their clunt and grapple
up jagged peaks that shoot through clouds
into the shocked and haloed air.

If the weakest slows, the strongest grows
responsible, much like when you were born:
hot and bothered, you heard bad bongos
and withdrew your raw body from the verge;
so they took up the slack as you dandled
at the wrong end of your string, puffing
and wedging and pulling you back
to teeter and totter on this edge.

Lagan Weir

The way things are going
    there'll be no quick fix, no turning
back the way that flock of starlings
    skirls back on itself, then swerves forward,
swabbing and scrawling the shell-pink
    buffed sky, while I stand in two minds
on this scuffed bridge leaning over
    the fudged river that slooshes its dark way
to open harbours and the glistering sea.

Like flak from fire, a blizzard of evacuees,
    that hula-hooping sky-swarm of starlings
swoops and loops the dog-rose sky,
    while any way I look the writing's
on the wall. I watch the hurly-burlyed,
    humdrummed traffic belch to a stop,
fugging, clacking, charring the clotted air,
    making it clear things are going to get
a whole lot worse before they get better.

That flickered, fluttered hurry-scurry
    of starlings sweeps left, then swishes right
through the violet sky while I huddle
    and huff, with a dove in one ear saying
look the other way, a hawk in the other
    braying self-righteous fury. It's hard
not to turn back to a time when one look
    at you and I knew things were going to get
a whole lot better before they'd get worse.

That hue and cry, those hurricanes
    of starlings swoosh and swirl their fractals
over towers, hotels, hospitals, flyovers,

catamarans, city-dwellers, passers-through,
    who might as well take a leap and try following
after that scatter-wheeling circus of shadows
    as slowly turn and make their dark way
homeward, never slowing, not knowing
    the way things are going.

On a Weekend Break in a Political Vacuum

To bugger off completely and drive north,
the breaking ocean on one side a tide
of greenblack rucks and rollings, with sea-blown
buoys and blue-starred water-lights pointing
the car beneath a V of whooper swans
gliding into the hoar-lit horizon — this is
her chance to blow out and clear the cobwebs
from her oblong desk and daylong circle
of managers, usernames, traffic and troubles,
the live death toll of the ten o'clock news.

Now the blues are low, and a bright red pouffe
in the rented backroom, with magazines
and the sprawl of Pacific Island nudes
in a greenwood frame entwine to snuffle
the harangue and ruckle of the workplace.
She inhales the dusk-scented air, then blows
it out, eyes closed in woollywarm jim-jams
with iced whiskey, magazines and the crash-
splashed, long, withdrawing roar of the sea
rasping behind the loose-rattled windows.

She drifts out of mind and feels the hurdy-
gurdy glare of the mall's special offers
on bright brands, travel agents' discounts
on the time of your life, as she sifts through
rayon and cashmere clothes stalls with fast hands.
In a perse and umber skirt she moves
through cottoned lawns of snow, or through
tansy-bloomed hills in a rose and cyan dress,
or by the dawn sea in a champagne-pink
gown after the Easter dance is over.

She feels the twilit roust of the ocean
as the chill-out blues and Gauguin print
beauties become phantoms, free from themselves,
drifting over hills, over the bedevilled sea.
She follows but falls, into the bedevilled sea,
sinking like a feather on an idle sea breeze
blown hither and thither through shoal-
motioned memories of other weekend
breaks by cockled shores, waving to her father
who disappears over sandblown dunes.

She nestles snugly, breathing in again,
free from the city mob's wolf whistles
and soon she is ago-go, ebbed and flowed
through light shallows, drifting in a lukewarm
lull until pulled down by colder currents
past the sharks of lost chances, the dogfish
of shame, coral thrones and the tepid tongues
of jilted lovers on her skin as she falls
through blackgreen sea-wrack and the gallery
of her days to rest on a bed of scuttled bones.

So often, this bellyache and boo-hoo,
this fall from bustle into soft bubbles
of self-regard where the headless chicken-
like rampage of her days dissolves into easy-
listening nights, while outside are militias,
lead levels, diplomacy and logistics
slowing executions and aid, and Aids,
migrations on twenty-four-hour broadcast,
temperature gauges and rice mountains,
serrating winds among the modified barley.

She accuses herself: as it is with the food
that awaits her, served with speed in a bright
labelled box (always that first bite's stomach-
melting dream chews to cardboard and carcass,
like a drunken one-night stand's aftermath
rising to a seasickness which empties,
utterly empties, so that she winds up
seeking the comfort of warm easy things —
the chilled blues and brightly-boxed food
that awaits her), so it is with her mind.

Still, she seeks amity by letting her head go
where it will, through the door and away from
the night to seek release by flushed coastlines
in a rising beryl dawn. She feels the coddle
of tawny skin, the tang of privet and firethorn,
the exhilaration of the city's nightlights
seen from a hill with low music from car
windows winding, melting from the hillway
into the chrysanthemum air like long-
winged sweepers over gardens drenched in May.

Why shouldn't she desire vast and headspun
centuries and catalogues of many-mooded
music caged within a prim pocket box,
or self-enhancing clothes, perfect colour
definitions on wide-framed screens, the glow
of bungalows on wild November nights,
fusions of style and functionality, cars with
womb-like interiors that take her, born again,
to the poplar groves of August, or Pacific
Island myths in dog-eared travel brochures?

She drifts, skimming her way over the deer-
grass hills and Sierra redwoods until sea winds
catch and sieve her through cirrus-scuffed skies,
as she swifts to a peak and then plummets
to a desert stalked by bone-caged phantoms,
infant guerillas, vector-borne disease
and the 6,500 Africans who died of Aids
today as others will tomorrow. She wakens
to gas-fired bars with a half-drained Powers
and ice smudging the piled-high magazines:

Country Interiors, Nuclear's Second Wind,
State of Fear, Time, Kiss and Tell, Twin Terrors,
OK, Hello, Another World is Possible.
She lights up and listens to house sparrows
skitter in the eaves as a male checks its nestlings,
then jumps the nest to spread his tawny wings,
swooping down to a bluebirds' cove
where it pecks a fledgling's head until dead —
skreak-screeching, wing-beating, beak threshing
open six speckled ash-grey newlaid eggs.

If she could only catch hold of herself
or seize each pulsed wave and mazed aftermath
twisting through her mind, she might know
what to do, who to be, the way things are.
But everything glitters for an instant
and then snuffs it. She's running out of breath,
chasing windblown leaves that are autumned
at a touch: flakes of promise bloomfalling
in a motion of mixed motives, ferris-wheeling
the nothing of death, the death of nothing.

She says: Tell that to the intern with electrodes
at his temples in an anonymous concrete
basement on the outskirts of the city
targeted by a trillion dollar war machine;
or the tiny man hooked below a white
transit van with his skin sned to turnip,
his cramped children left continents behind;
the infected girl watching mosquitoes
bite her newborn son, waiting for raping
dawn-raiders wielding European guns.

Her friends tell her to get out more and learn
to love the shale and spray of the coast's
frowsty smacks of fast mazarine air
under the peach-blushed and petrel-charged sky.
And so she will walk through wind-rushed
barley, angelica and high groves,
hoping to glimpse the glint of sorrel-
coated horses galloping through unhedged
greens towards the blue surveilled horizons
hearing river water running underground.

In the greenwood framed Gauguin print's
shades of peace and gentle violation
a youth lifts up tawny-skinned arms
to pluck fruit from a writhing blue tree,
just as these poplars lift their green-fired leaves
to pluck the sun from a cornflower sky.
There is no Law saying cursed is the ground,
although the ground is cursed. She will savour
sea-blown salt spray as soldiers police their
barracks below a gobsmacked garnet sky.

As if a child over a clump of broken dolls,
hoping to unmurder, she'll watch the endless
waves reach their limits and she will walk
through the phantom air, its contagion of blue,
as starlings flusker through changing skies
to alight on numbered trees, bursting out
of themselves, straining to reach up to
the death-flare of the sun, which multiplies.
But, for now, she lies back to sleep and dream,
enjoy the weekend. There is work to do.

Death by Preventable Poverty

Three seconds passed, another one dead,
I walked past violets and windflowers,
cowbind, eglantine, moonlight-coloured may
and ivy serpentine snaking as I railed
after the epiphanies were over,
reeled among white cups and clover,
flag flowers, riverbuds awaiting the hail
that will hail on oxslips, bluebells looking to stay
the west-blown cyclone, these galled hours
and phantoms, children, flustered in my head,
yellow, and black, and pale, and red.

Harvest

1

The two of them were forever banging
on about keeping your conscience spick and span
as a scoured kitchen surface and grafting
bone-hard in life's grim dockyard, each time giving
it everything. If a peeler took one through
the cummerbund outside the secret policeman's
dancehall, or Marks and Spencers blew
its windows one hundred and seventy-
five feet in the air to rain down arrows on the newly
disfigured, they'd be livid if I didn't wash my hands.

Maybe this is why I'm licking my chops
at the thought of microwaved trays
of pork bangers and bleached potato slops,
driving to Killymoon through hay fields and green
fields decked with pat-caked cows;
why my parents have turned into odd
truisms, viruses mutating through the thin streams
of my brain into screenplays of low-beamed
corners in dancehalls; why I'm wondering how
two free wills become two peas in a pod.

2

Half-baked under the spalding orange rays,
they birl and dunt their pitchforks in the fum.
A horse's scream of rain will soon come
and wash all this away, but now the women lay

the table with hot boxty bread. She sucks an orange finger.
His breeks are ripped to flitterjigs
as he snuffles his neb and spies the stoppled eaves
of her breasts, before gobbing a pure emerald yinger.

And he can't help but think
of her in a bool of earth-swell, the hurt
weaver's kiss of her tights, raising her skirts
against the clay-baked orange-brown turf bink.

Now they trudge back along the oaten
shingle, a bunch of branny-faced boys in jouked
breeks by the reed-kissed bebble of a brook.
It's hard to judge when the sky will be opened.

3

Trigger-happy tomcats and hornets jet
into the sun, their motherloads dead set
on the clay-baked cities of Iraq, as I sit
back and order an overcooked frozen fillet
of salmon with hard potatoes and spoon-
mashed turnip with my parents at Killymoon's
nearest hotel, my newborn son on my breast
with my Ma insisting, despite my cloud-dark frown,
that a brandy-soaked sugar cube is best
for traumatic nights as the rain knuckles down.

Someday I might return and tell him this
is near where they met, where they might have been
married, as the rain batters remorseless
on watchtowers, their camouflaged polytetrafluoroethylene,

as I lead him down the road of falling
hazels and vetch, finger to finger
until he lets go and leaves me by a reed-shushing
brook under the sky's orange plumes,
the fallout winds and elder
stealing kisses on the road to Killymoon.

After this Storm Blows Over

If I make it the weather will coat the country
in an angel-cloaked clabber and the house
will fill to burst with drink and blather
while I eavesdrop by the window,
watching you dink and shuffle, listening
to everything with thistle-pink ears pricked
for drain guzzle, smoke plume, feather ruffle,
frost thaw, duffel rustle, water draw —
the aerial of your bobble hat glistening.

Laganside

I cannot call back the time, lasso the millions
of minutes by the scruff of their scrawny
wee seconds, or knock out the lost years,
bop the back of their heads and bale
them into a getaway van that will welly it
to a warehouse where time is put right
by a crack team of agents in tandem
with a renegade but brilliant neurobiologist.
No, the missing months are truly missing,
marooned, cut adrift, left for bye-bye to dry
out in the wreck of themselves, then stalk
an undead and hollow land forever thirsting.

Anyway, it's been ages since I last happened
by this riverside walkway, where the dead
wood reeked by weather is spring cleaned.
And I never learned the name of anything,
but it's nice to see no one's ripped the plants
out by their roots and burnt and pissed over
the empty burned space where the ripped-up,
pissed-on plants used to be. And it really is
great to stick on names that you've heard
to whatever you like without caring. So,
along this riverside pathway that snakes
through the city, this laminate lagoon,

buckeyes and rose of Sharon bushes occupy
snowberry banks, restharrow and gillyflowers
garland bamboo trunks and sapodillas,
while a lotusbird perches to coo-coo
with currawongs and chuck-will's-widows,
orangequits and greenshanks tra-la twittering,
tittering and tottering on high branches

of lacquer trees, getting liquored on ylang
ylang, oakmoss, dragon's blood and thyme.
But tiring of this I ask my better half
if she knows what anything is, and she quotes to me:
'Happiness is good health and bad memory.'

A man screams. I jitter. But he's shouting
at his pupils tinned in a pointy-headed
rowboat, and I'm almost insulted,
given the streets are full of men who would
think nothing of going right up to a tiger
lily and scrunching its corolla, who'd shoot
the crows for target practice if they could take out
their guns; and so, I shouldn't exaggerate,
given that if a duck even tried to quack-
quack in that water, it would be a stone-
dead mallard before long; given that beneath
the bokey fudged mulch you can see 3D

nightmares of chains and pulleys, high school
bullies, trolleys, satanic creepy crawlies,
a Black & Decker angle grinder, outstanding
debt reminders, buckled pushchairs, threadbare
pink and olive striped deckchairs, moustachioed
schoolmasters, startled newscasters introducing
shots of headshots, roadblocks, deadlocks,
English cocks and Irish Jocks, mutilated livestock,
a timer's tick-tock, confused with the cistern's drip-
drop, keeping you up to panic at a midnight knock-
knock, which is just a drunk neighbour who thought
his missus must ive change da fuckin front-dure lock.

Anyway, while all this flows towards Belfast Lough
it's not exactly Xanadu above water either,
not quite Honolulu, when above and beyond
the trees all I can see are weed-nooked rust-yards
fighting for space with erect hotels and pearly
office centres, tall cranes stalking everywhere:
tower cranes, hydraulic cranes, cranes for all terrain
policing thin streets in bright-sprayed armatures,
lording it over buildings like a supreme new race,
looking towards their unused elders hung
in sorrow in the dockyards to the east; whether
in sympathy, or saying up yours, I'm not sure.

Closer to the riverside, terraced doors keep
their mouths shut and children are clamped
in by barricade from this steep fall of river-
bank and clean public walkway, though buttered
faces size me up from behind a useless wall,
cursing the river's limitations, my trespass,
this tourist sprawl. But then, moving onward,
by a cream call centre, a sunbed-skinned sales team
have finished their shift and stream through
the fence-gate to traipse toward happy hour
promotions, black power retro-nights, their navel
studs and highlights sparked by waterlight.

But these airs, this river, these sights have not
been to me some happy-clappy totem,
nor a masochistic home-truth tucked away
in the dark corner of my room mid the nee-
nar drone or bling-bling neon of foreign
towns and cities where I've ordered Pad
Thai noodles and drawn the blinds to dwell

on the blank page at the end of 'Ovid
in Tomis'. It's just I've never come down
since these tracks were laid, and this path
is like my tongue after biting a Pink Lady
cling-wrapped in a thin film of cellophane.

Of course, this happens all the time: you walk
up to your neighbour and note his nostril
hairs, dimples, pocks, scars, cheeks and creviced
chin; then five minutes later you catch his nut-
brown eyes in the light and all the features
of his face fuse into something whole but shifting
like this river; or you run your hardly-haired
fingers over the deep blue tiles that line your bath
and soon they're pigeon's neck or tortoiseshell,
turquoise flashing eyes on a peacock's wing;
so it's unsurprising I'm a bit bamboozled
by this crash and build of trees and concrete

under ice-blue skies, which are hardly ice-
blue, but electric, kingfisher, and airforce
blue stretched over this crocodilic river
preying straight for the lough's open maw
to leave behind all guarantees; horse chestnuts
and hazel trees; the roadways' injured circuitry;
wheelie-bins and empties; wideboys hawking
blow to the gothic daughters of the haute
bourgeoisie; and my better half and me
below clouds that taper the city's spires,
cupolas, scaffolding, lithe birds of origami.

No wonder I'm astray, a little bit this way
and that way, for the dockyards and ghettoes

look like a grey-quiffed and tattooed uncle
intensely line dancing on a hot night-
club floor, thinking he might yet score,
like I've been caught with my guard down
by this dizzy glint and easy rapture
of poplar and clover, wire-fence and river
flooding towards the basin's broken jaws
as if hit-and-running from a crime scene,
though flushed and peach-blushed with pleasure
at the prospect of coming to a head,

having it out for once and forever
as the missing months and years dredge
past the massage of washed-out slogans,
sleek towers, ghosted union buildings,
the river overrunning its own ledge
to find itself played out in a final flush
into open seas, under drizzled rain,
while the sky arrests an outbound plane,
and my better half lags behind to savour
the shifting terrain, leaving me to find
our way back to the streets, knowing
I'll never leave here, or come back again.

Acknowledgements

Many thanks to the Arts Council of Northern Ireland, from which I received an award under the Support for Individual Artists Programme in 2005.

Acknowledgements are due to the editors of *Éire-Ireland* and *The Edinburgh Review*, in which some of these poems, or early versions of them, have appeared. 'Saturday Morning' was included in *The Yellow Nib: The Literary Journal of the Seamus Heaney Centre for Poetry* (Blackstaff Press), 'There' and 'In Her Room on a Light-kissed Afternoon' in *Magnetic North: The Emerging Poets* (Lagan Press), and 'For What We Are About To Receive' in *Taste: An Anthology of Poetry About Food* (Clan-U Press).

I'd also like to thank Ciaran Carson and Peter Fallon, along with the friends and colleagues who have helped and supported me over the past three years. Warmest thanks for their indulgence are due to my family, and especially to my wife.